GEOFACTS

BIOME

GEO FACTS

Izzi Howell

Crabtree Publishing Company
www.crabtreebooks.com

Crabtree Publishing Company
www.crabtreebooks.com
1-800-387-7650

Published in Canada
Crabtree Publishing
616 Welland Avenue
St. Catharines, ON
L2M 5V6

Published in the United States
Crabtree Publishing
PMB 59051
350 Fifth Ave, 59th Floor
New York, NY 10118

Published in 2018 by CRABTREE PUBLISHING COMPANY.

First published in 2017 by The Watts Publishing Group
Copyright © The Watts Publishing Group 2017

Author: Izzi Howell

Editors: Izzi Howell, Petrice Custance

Design: Rocket Design (East Anglia) Ltd

Editorial director: Kathy Middleton

Proofreader: Angela Kaelberer

Prepress technician: Abigail Smith

Print and production coordinator: Margaret Amy Salter

Photographs
Alamy: John Michaels 12; iStock: AVTG 6t, Marina_Poushkina 20t; NASA: NASA/GSFC/LaRC/JPL, MISR Team 24, Jacques Descloitres, MODIS Land Science Team 28l; Shutterstock: marilyn barbone 6b, FotoRequest 7tl, Tom Reichner 7tr, Wolfilser 7c, Menno Schaefer 7b, f11photo 8, Onnes 9t, BGSmith 9c, Michael Stokes 9b, Stephane Bidouze 10, feathercollector 11l, Tanor 11tr, ChameleonsEye 11cr, Ryan M. Bolton 11br, Michael Zysman 13tl, Eduardo Rivero 13tr and br, esdeem 13bl, AndreAnita 14t, angie oxley 14b, EastVillage Images 15t, marco 15b, Patrick Poendl 16t, Adwo 16b, hagit berkovich 17t, Zack Frank 17tc, EcoPrint 17bc, Stanislav Fosenbauer 17b, Pichugin Dmitry 18, Bildagentur Zoonar GmbH 19tl, boombox 19tr, inavanhateren 19bl, photoff 19br, Vladimir Melnik 20tc, Nicram Sabod 20bc, Jeff McGraw 20b, Volodymyr Goinyk 21t, vladsilver 21b, Federico Rostagno 22, Michael Bogner 23l, Rich Carey 23tr, VisionDive 23cr, Yory Frenklakh 23br, worldswildlifewonders 25l, LauraD 25c, Ethan Daniels 25r, Elena Elisseeva 26, Birute Vijeikiene 27t, underworld 27c, cristalvi 27b, Oleg Znamenskiy 28r, Lachlan von Nubia 29t, Bildagentur Zoonar GmbH 29bl and br, Techtype 4–5, 6–7, 10–11, 16–17, 20.

All design elements from Shutterstock: song_mi, Sherry Zaat, labzazuza, Rhoeo, skelos, mamita, Kazakova Maryia, Victor Du Bois, Alfonso de Tomas, Spreadthesign, NoPainNoGain, Natali Snailcat, Merkushev Vasiliy, Snez, BlueRingMedia, Aleksey Vanin, FrimuFilms and ARTYuCREATIVE.

Every attempt has been made to clear copyright. Should there be any inadvertent omission, please apply to the publisher for rectification.

Printed in the USA/122019/BG20171102

Library and Archives Canada Cataloguing in Publication

Howell, Izzi, author
    Biome geo facts / Izzi Howell.

(Geo facts)
Includes index.
Issued in print and electronic formats.
ISBN 978-0-7787-4381-1 (hardcover).--
ISBN 978-0-7787-4396-5 (softcover).--
ISBN 978-1-4271-2014-4 (HTML)

    1. Biotic communities--Juvenile literature. 2. Ecology--Juvenile literature. I. Title.

QH541.14.H69 2018   j577   C2017-906899-7
                                         C2017-906900-4

Library of Congress Cataloging-in Publication Data

Names: Howell, Izzi, author.
Title: Biome geo facts / Izzi Howell.
Description: New York, New York : Crabtree Publishing Company, [2018
Series: Geo facts | Includes index.
Identifiers: LCCN 2017050649 (print) | LCCN 2017055325 (ebook) |
  ISBN 9781427120144 (Electronic HTML) |
  ISBN 9780778743811 (reinforced library binding) |
  ISBN 9780778743965 (pbk.)
Subjects: LCSH: Biotic communities--Juvenile literature. | Habitat (Ecology)--Juvenile literature. | Ecology--Juvenile literature.
Classification: LCC QH541.14 (ebook) | LCC QH541.14 .H69 2018 (print) | DDC 577.8/2--dc23
LC record available at https://lccn.loc.gov/2017050649

Contents

What is a Biome?

Biomes are natural areas on Earth that have the same climate, landscape, plants, and animals. They can be on land or in water. There are many different **habitats** and **ecosystems** within each biome.

The map on the right shows the main biomes of the world.

- Temperate forest – page 6
- Taiga – page 6
- Tropical rain forest – page 10
- Grassland – page 14
- Savanna – page 14
- Desert – page 16
- Tundra – page 20
- Ice – page 20
- Ocean – page 22
- Freshwater – page 26

FOCUS ON **Yosemite** (page 8)

FOCUS ON **The Amazon Rain forest** (page 12)

Habitats

A habitat is the area where a certain plant or animal lives. For example, the habitat of a tawny owl is the trees in temperate forests. Some species have their habitat in several biomes. The African elephant moves between rain forests, savannas, and even deserts.

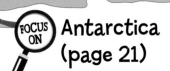

FOCUS ON **Antarctica** (page 21)

Ecosystems

An ecosystem is the relationship between all living things in an area. Living things can be connected by food chains or by their behavior, such as the way insects help to pollinate flowers. If one plant or animal in an ecosystem disappears, it affects all the other living things in the area.

Adaptations

Animals and plants are **adapted** to the conditions of the biome where they live. These can be physical adaptations, such as fins, or behavioral adaptations, such as **migration**. We can see similar adaptations in different animals in the same biome.

FOCUS ON **The Serengeti** (page 15)

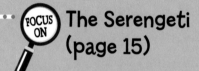

FOCUS ON **The Nile River** (page 28)

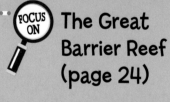

FOCUS ON **The Great Barrier Reef** (page 24)

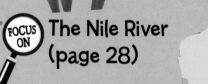

FOCUS ON **The Sahara Desert** (page 18)

Forests

Forests cover around one-third of land on Earth. There are three main types of forest biome: taiga, temperate, and rainforest (see pages 10-11).

The taiga has rocky soil with few nutrients.

 Taiga

 Temperate

Differences

Although the taiga and temperate forests are both areas with many trees, there are several important differences between them.

	TAIGA	TEMPERATE
LOCATION	Far north	Northern and southern hemispheres
NEARBY BIOMES	Between the tundra and temperate forests	Found to the south of the taiga
CLIMATE	Cold and snowy for most of the year, cool in summer	Changes with the seasons—hot in summer and cold in the winter

*Plants such as bluebells grow in the **fertile** soil of temperate forests. The soil is fertilized by the decomposing fallen leaves of **deciduous** trees.*

Seasons

Both taiga and temperate forests have separate seasons with different temperatures. The taiga has long winters and short summers. Temperate forests have seasons of equal length.

Deciduous trees

The majority of trees in temperate forests are deciduous. Their leaves turn orange or yellow in autumn and fall off in winter. The trees regrow their leaves in spring. Deciduous trees get the energy and nutrients they need to regrow their leaves from the increased hours of sunlight as well as the rich soil of the temperate forests.

spring

summer

autumn

winter

Animal and plant adaptations

Winter is the most challenging season for forest animals and plants. In the taiga, winter is so cold that many animals migrate or hibernate until spring. In the milder temperate forests, animals often hide extra food in summer and autumn to eat later during the snowy winter, when there is less food available.

*The brown snowshoe hare grows white fur in winter for **camouflage**.*

The fir tree has a cone shape so that snow falls off it, which stops branches from breaking under the weight of the snow.

The red squirrel buries extra food or hides it in holes in trees.

Evergreen trees

Most trees in the taiga are **evergreen**. Evergreen trees don't drop their leaves in autumn. The leaves stay green all year and are replaced gradually, so trees don't need to regrow all their leaves in spring. This would require energy and nutrients that are hard to come by in the dark, rocky taiga.

7

FOCUS ON

Yosemite

Yosemite National Park is in California, on the west coast of the United States. It contains large areas of taiga and temperate forests, including groups of giant sequoia trees.

FACT FILE

📊 SIZE
1,168 square miles (3,026 square km)

📋 NATIONAL PARK SINCE
1890

🔺 HIGHEST POINT
13,114 feet (3,997 m)

Landscape

Located in the Sierra Nevada mountain range, Yosemite has a rocky terrain with high cliffs, valleys, and canyons. Several of its dramatic rock formations were formed by ancient **glaciers** that have melted away. There are many rivers and lakes among the trees.

Above the treeline at Yosemite (the highest point at which trees can grow), there is only exposed rock, with very few plants.

Climate

Overall, the climate of Yosemite is warm in summer and cold in winter. There is often snow on the ground from November until March. High mountain peaks experience much colder temperatures than lower areas of the park.

Sequoias

Giant sequoia trees grow on the slopes of mountains in Yosemite. These giant evergreen trees are the largest trees on Earth and can live to be over 3,000 years old. They provide shelter and food for many forest animals, such as squirrels.

People

The Yosemite area was inhabited by Native Americans for thousands of years, but many were killed or forced to move in the 1800s.

Today, Yosemite receives over 3.8 million visitors every year, many of whom enjoy activities such as hiking.

American black bear

The American black bear lives in forests across North America. In Yosemite, the bears are found in high, wooded areas that are far from tourist trails.

thick fur to protect against the cold

OMNIVORE diet that guarantees food all year round

good sense of smell to find food among the trees

! Trees in the sequoia family can grow to heights of 377 feet (115 m), which is taller than the Statue of Liberty!

sharp claws for climbing trees to find food

HIBERNATES to survive low temperatures and poor food supply

9

Rain Forests

Rain forests are warm, wet forests that are found on both sides of the equator in Africa, South America, Asia, and Oceania. Many different species of plants and animals live in the rainforest biome.

Clouds filled with rain often form above the tops of rainforest trees.

Climate

Rain forests, like most areas near the equator, have a warm climate. There is heavy rain all year round. Some of the rain is brought by ocean winds, and some is water that has **evaporated** from the leaves of rainforest plants.

Rain forest

Central American

Amazon

Layers

The rainforest biome is divided into four layers. Animal and plant life, as well as amounts of sunlight, vary from layer to layer.

EMERGENT LAYER
A few very tall trees grow up into the emergent layer, which can be over 164 feet (50 m) from the forest floor.

CANOPY LAYER
The top branches of trees intertwine to form the canopy layer, where most animals live.

UNDERSTORY
Large-leaved plants grow in the understory, which receives little light.

FOREST FLOOR
The roots of tall trees and vines are found on the dark forest floor. It is home to insects and large mammals that cannot climb into the canopy layer.

The thick canopy of trees and plants in the rain forest means that it can take a drop of rain ten minutes to fall from the canopy to the forest floor.

Animal and plant adaptations

Rainforest animals and plants are adapted to suit the conditions of the layer in which they live. Tall trees have their roots in the dark forest floor but grow to great heights, searching for sunlight to make energy. As most food can be found in the canopy layer, many animals live high up and move by jumping, flying, or swinging.

Air plants (epiphytes) grow on trees in the sunny canopy layer. They get moisture and nutrients from the air and rain instead of the soil.

Southeast Asia

The spider monkey has a long tail that can hold on to branches, freeing up its hands to pick food.

Australia

The Wallace's flying frog has thin membranes between its toes that help it glide through the air from tree to tree.

Congo River Basin

Madagascar

! Scientists think that around half of all known species of plants and animals on Earth live in the rainforest biome.

In just one area of the Panama rain forest, about the size of a football field, scientists have found 6,000 different insect species, including the Hercules beetle (above).

Biodiversity

Rain forests are one of the most **biodiverse** biomes on Earth. This means that they contain a very high number of different plant and animal species. Some scientists think that this is because each rainforest layer is a separate habitat, supporting many different types of living things.

The Amazon Rain Forest

The Amazon rain forest is found in northern South America. It is the largest rain forest in the world and spans nine countries, including Brazil, Colombia, and Peru.

FACT FILE

SIZE
2 million square miles (5.2 million square km)

AVERAGE RAINFALL PER YEAR
118 inches (3,000 mm)

AVERAGE TEMPERATURE
80°Fahrenheit (27°C)

The Amazon River

The Amazon River is about 4,000 miles (6,437 km) long and flows through the area north of the Amazon rain forest. Trees grow right up to the river banks. Some rainforest animals come down to the river to catch fish and drink.

Oxygen

When plants **photosynthesize,** or make food, they release oxygen. The trees and plants in the Amazon rain forest produce 20 percent of all oxygen on Earth, giving the rain forest the nickname "the lungs of the Earth."

People

Over 30 million people live in and around the Amazon rain forest. There are a few large cities and many small farming towns. More than 350 nations of **Indigenous** peoples still live a traditional lifestyle, partly depending on the rain forest for food and shelter.

These Tucano men are hunting on the Amazon River in a traditional canoe carved from a rainforest tree. The Tucano are Indigenous peoples who mainly live in Colombia.

Number of species

Rain forests are known for their biodiversity, but the Amazon rain forest has an astonishing number of species. 10 percent of all species known to humans can be found in this rain forest, including 40,000 plant species, 1,300 bird species, and 2.5 million species of insect.

Deforestation

Over 17 percent of the Amazon rain forest has been destroyed in the past fifty years. Trees are cut down for wood and the land is cleared for farmland and mining.

*Many Amazon species, such as the red-faced bald uakari monkey (above), are **endangered.** The increasing loss of their habitat means they have difficulty finding food or shelter.*

Keel-billed toucan

The keel-billed toucan is adapted for life high in the trees of the rainforest canopy.

sharp beak to cut through thick-skinned fruit

long beak to reach fruit on branches that are too small to support its weight

bright colors for camouflage near brightly colored flowers and leaves

strong claws that face forward and backward to grasp branches

Giant anteater

The giant anteater lives on the dark, damp rainforest floor.

good sense of smell to find food in dark areas

good swimmer to travel across water to find food

large sticky tongue that sweeps up many ants at once

large claws to break open anthills on the forest floor and fight off PREDATORS such as jaguars

Grasslands and Savannas

Grasslands and savannas are biomes that are mainly covered in grass and low plants. They are found on every continent except Antarctica.

Differences

Grasslands and savannas differ in their temperature and rainfall. Different types of plants can be found in each biome.

	GRASSLAND	SAVANNA
TEMPERATURE	Cold winters and hot summers	Warm all year round
RAINFALL	Generally dry, with some rain in spring	Heavy rain during the rainy season, none during the dry season
PLANTS	Many different types of grass with deep roots to hold the plant in place during strong winds	Grass and scattered trees and shrubs, which provide shade

Animal adaptations

Grassland and savanna herbivores are adapted to eat different kinds of plants so that they don't eat too much of one type. Some are grazers, eating low grass and plants, and some are browsers, picking leaves and shoots from trees. Predators hunt in the open grassland, where there is nowhere for their **prey** to hide.

GRASSLANDS AND SAVANNAS
The giraffe has a long neck to reach leaves in tall trees.

GRASSLANDS
The American bison has large wide teeth that grind down tough grasses.

The Serengeti

The Serengeti is an area of grassland and savanna that spans nearly 12,000 square miles (30,000 square km) across the east of Africa. Its warm, dry season lasts for most of the year.

During the rainy season, migrating wildebeest and zebras feast on the bright green grass of the Serengeti.

Fires

Fires are common in the Serengeti during the dry season. These fires burn down young trees and stop forests from forming. Although the top parts of the grass plants are burned away, their deep roots survive underground so the plants can grow back. The ash left by the fire fertilizes the soil.

Migration

Many animals in the Serengeti migrate to avoid the dry season and find grass to graze on. Over 1.5 million wildebeest and 200,000 zebras migrate every year, making it the largest land mammal migration on Earth.

Umbrella thorn

The umbrella thorn tree is adapted to live in dry areas of the Serengeti. Its leaves and seeds provide food for many animals.

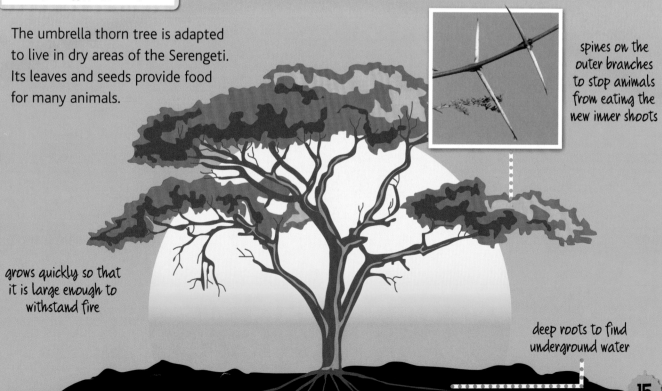

spines on the outer branches to stop animals from eating the new inner shoots

grows quickly so that it is large enough to withstand fire

deep roots to find underground water

Deserts

Deserts are dry areas with little rainfall. The desert biome covers around one-fifth of Earth's surface. Deserts can be found on every continent, including Antarctica.

Shrubs and palm trees grow around desert oases.

Temperatures

Most deserts have hot weather, but some deserts near the poles can be very cold. The world's largest desert, in Antarctica, is one of the coldest places on Earth, with an average temperature of -76°F (-60°C).

Great Basin

Chihuahuan

Sonoran

Desert

Sahara

Water

On average, deserts receive less than 10 inches (25 cm) of rain per year. Some deserts experience almost no rain at all. The only regular water supply in the desert is deep underground. This water sometimes comes to the surface as a spring, forming a lush **oasis.**

Atacama

Kalahari

Patagonia

Yes, there is a desert at the South Pole! You don't need sand for a desert— it just needs to be an area with no rain.

One part of the Atacama desert went over 14 years without rain in the early 20th century.

Antarctica

16

Day and night

As there isn't enough water vapor in the dry air for clouds to form and block the heat from the Sun, daytime temperatures can be very high. At night, the temperature drops massively, as there are no clouds to trap the Sun's heat.

In the Sahara Desert, daytime temperatures are over 104°F (40°C) but can drop below 32°F (0°C) at night.

104°

32°

Karakum

Gobi

Thar

Arabian

Great Sandy

Great Victoria

Animal and plant adaptations

Desert animals and plants are adapted to extreme temperatures and life with very little water. To keep cool, many desert animals are nocturnal, which means that they sleep during the hot day (often in underground burrows) and come out during the cool night. The roots of some desert plants travel up to 3 feet (1 m) underground to find moisture in the dry soil.

The fennec fox has large ears that radiate its body heat away to reduce sweating.

The saguaro cactus stores extra rainwater in its stem so that it can survive until the next rainfall.

The scorpion has a hard outer shell that keeps moisture in its body.

Landscape

Desert biomes can have sand, rocks, steep canyons, and tall mountains. Sometimes, desert winds blow loose sand into hills, known as dunes, and carve rocks into interesting shapes.

Uluru is a large rock formation in the desert of central Australia. It has great cultural importance to Indigenous peoples.

FOCUS ON

The Sahara Desert

The Sahara Desert is the largest hot desert in the world. It stretches across the north of Africa, taking up around a quarter of the continent.

FACT FILE

 SIZE
3.6 million square miles (9.4 million square km)

 AVERAGE RAINFALL PER YEAR
2.95 inches (7.5 cm)

 AVERAGE TEMPERATURE
(summer) **104°F (40°C)**

AVERAGE TEMPERATURE
(winter) **55°F (13°C)**

A Tuareg man leads his camels through the Sahara Desert in Algeria.

Mountains

More than a quarter of the Sahara Desert is made up of high mountains and **plateaus**. On the northwest edge of the Sahara, the Atlas Mountains act as a barrier, blocking moisture from the Mediterranean Sea and the Atlantic Ocean.

Subtropical desert

Most of the moisture in the air falls as rain in the warm tropical rain forests along the equator. By the time this air reaches the Sahara Desert, it contains very little water, so there is no rainfall.

People

The Sahara Desert is home to Indigenous peoples such as the Tuareg and the Toubou. These peoples live as nomadic livestock herders, living in tents and moving around the desert to find land for their animals to graze. They trade and pick up supplies at the small **settlements** that have been built around oases.

Sandstorms

In the spring, strong desert winds sometimes pick up dust and sand and whirl them around in a spiral, creating a sandstorm. These sandstorms can travel large distances, choking people and animals in their path.

Wadis

Dry riverbeds called wadis can be found across the Sahara Desert. In the rare event of rain, wadis can fill up with water in an instant.

Plants

Shrubs and acacia trees in the Sahara Desert have long roots to reach underground water. Tall palm trees grow around desert oases, giving shade to shorter plants.

Dromedary camel

The dromedary camel lives across north Africa, the Middle East, and Australia. It is perfectly suited to hot, dry desert conditions.

thick eyebrows and eyelashes stop sand from entering the eye

hump stores up to 79 pounds (36 kg) of fat, which can break down into water and energy when none is available

can drink up to 5 gallons (19 liters) per minute

tough lips to eat thorny desert plants

rarely sweats

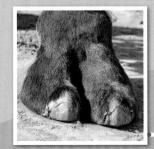

wide hooves to balance on rock and sand

19

Tundra and Ice

The poles are the northernmost and southernmost points on Earth. There is no land at the North Pole. The closest land is the icy tundra in the Arctic Circle. The South Pole is on the continent of Antarctica.

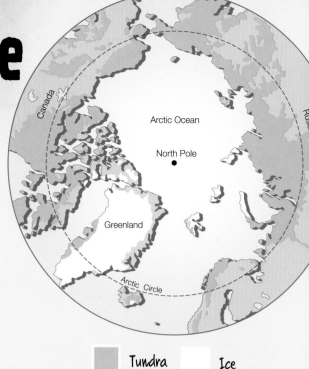

Canada
Arctic Ocean
North Pole
Russia
Greenland
Arctic Circle

Tundra   Ice

Tundra

The tundra is cold and windy with very few trees. It is covered in snow during the long winter, and most of the soil beneath the surface is permafrost, which remains frozen year round.

Seasons

The poles and the Arctic Circle have short summers with 24 hours of sunlight each day. During the winter, there are 24 hours of darkness. The average summer temperature in the tundra is 37-54°F (3-12°C), but in winter, the average temperature falls to -29°F (-34°C).

When it is winter in the Arctic tundra, it is summer in Antarctica. This is because they are in different hemispheres.

The surface water that isn't absorbed by the frozen tundra soil forms bogs in summer, attracting birds and insects.

Animal and plant adaptations

Tundra plants and animals are adapted to the long winters and extreme cold. Plants have shallow roots to avoid the permafrost and short growing seasons to make the most of the summer sunshine. As in the taiga, many tundra animals migrate or hibernate to survive the freezing winters, but some animals have adapted to life in the deep snow.

The tufted saxifrage grows close to the ground where the air is warmer and there is less wind.

The musk ox uses its strong hooves to dig through snow to find plants hidden underneath.

The caribou has hollow hairs that trap air against its body, providing extra insulation against the cold.

Antarctica

Antarctica is the coldest, windiest, and driest continent on Earth. Its conditions are too extreme for most animals and plants.

In some areas, high rocky mountains rise above the sheet of ice that covers Antarctica.

Soil and plants

Nearly all of Antarctica is covered in a layer of ice that is about 1 mile (1.6 km) thick. As the soil is buried so deeply beneath the ice, the only plants that can survive in this environment are mosses and lichens, which absorb water and nutrients from the air.

Land and Sea

The largest land animals that live on Antarctica are tiny insects. However, many species of fish and mammal live in the seas around Antarctica. Some come on land to rest and breed.

Emperor penguin

The emperor penguin lives in the water and on land along the coast of Antarctica. Its adaptations help it to survive in extreme cold temperatures, as low as -76°F (-60°C).

thick body fat and several layers of feathers to protect against the cold

streamlined body and powerful flippers for swimming

huddle together in groups to conserve heat

strong claws to grip ice

21

Oceans

Oceans are the largest biome on Earth, covering three-quarters of the globe. They vary in depth and temperature, with different plants and animals living in each zone.

This is the coast of the Caribbean Sea. Seas are small areas of oceans that are close to land.

Temperatures

We can divide the oceans into three types based on their temperature: polar, temperate, and tropical. Water depth can also affect temperature.

	TEMPERATURE
POLAR	Under 50°F (10°C)
TEMPERATE	50-64°F (10-18°C)
TROPICAL	Above 64°F (18°C)

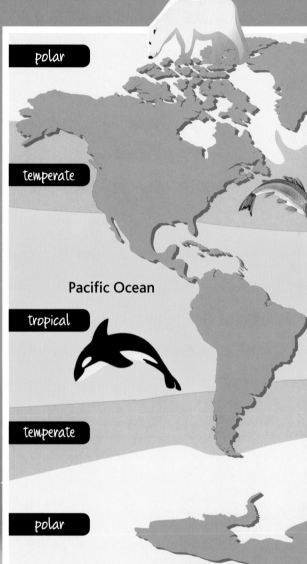

polar

temperate

Pacific Ocean

tropical

temperate

polar

Depth

Near the surface, the ocean is well-lit, warm, and teeming with life. There is less and less light as the water gets deeper. The deepest parts of the ocean are cold and pitch-black, with huge amounts of pressure from the weight of the water above.

Movement

Wind causes waves on the surface of the water. **Currents** form when parts of the ocean with different temperatures and salt levels meet. Along the coast, the sea level rises and falls because of tides caused by the gravitational pull of the Moon and the Sun.

Arctic Ocean

Indian Ocean

Atlantic Ocean

Southern Ocean

Animal adaptations

All ocean animals are adapted to live underwater, where there is no air. Fish and invertebrates, such as coral, absorb oxygen from the water. Ocean mammals and reptiles fill their large lungs with air from the surface before diving underwater. Many ocean animals have **streamlined** bodies and fins to push them through the water.

The octopus can swim or use its legs to walk along the ocean floor.

The great white shark has gills that absorb oxygen from seawater and release carbon dioxide.

*The Atlantic wolffish produces **antifreeze** to keep its blood flowing in near-freezing waters.*

Plants

Ocean plants such as seaweed and sea grass do not have roots as land plants do. They absorb water through their leaves and their stalk. However, they do photosynthesize, which means they must live in sunny water near the surface.

Kelp forests grow in shallow temperate water. They provide shelter and food for many ocean animals.

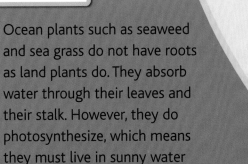

FOCUS ON

The Great Barrier Reef

The Great Barrier Reef is the largest coral reef on Earth. It is located off the northeast coast of Australia and can be seen from space.

FACT FILE

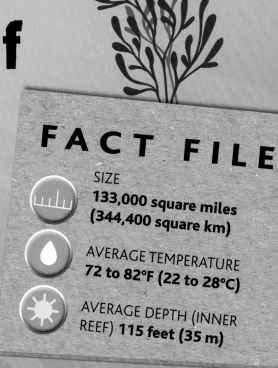

SIZE
133,000 square miles (344,400 square km)

AVERAGE TEMPERATURE
72 to 82°F (22 to 28°C)

AVERAGE DEPTH (INNER REEF) 115 feet (35 m)

Coral reefs

Coral reefs form in shallow, clear, warm water. Although coral looks like a plant, it is actually the outer skeletons of thousands of tiny animals called polyps. Algae often grows on the surface of the coral, giving it a bright color.

The shape of the Great Barrier Reef can be seen from space.

Great Barrier Reef

Animals

Coral reefs are often known as the rain forests of the ocean, as they are incredibly biodiverse. Over 400 types of hard coral, 1,500 species of fish, 134 species of sharks and rays, and 30 types of marine mammals live in the Great Barrier Reef, all of which depend on each other to survive.

Types of reef

Barrier reefs, such as the Great Barrier Reef, are long reefs that form along a coastline, with deep water between the land and the reef. A coral atoll is a ring-shaped reef with shallow water in the center.

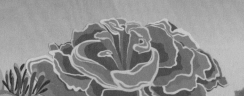

Islands

Sea birds rest and lay their eggs on islands in the Great Barrier Reef. Some of these islands are part of the continental shelf, the land underneath the ocean. Others are cays—small islands formed from sand that has settled on the reef.

People

Indigenous peoples and Torres Strait Islanders have fished and sailed around the Great Barrier Reef for tens of thousands of years. Today, the reef is a popular tourist destination, receiving two million tourists a year.

Threats

The future of the Great Barrier Reef is threatened by water pollution and overfishing. Rising water temperatures and acidity, caused by carbon dioxide in the atmosphere, are killing large amounts of coral. Without coral, other reef animals cannot survive.

The crown of thorns starfish preys on coral and can destroy large areas of coral reef.

Green sea turtle

Green sea turtles can be found in the Great Barrier Reef, as well as in the Atlantic, Pacific, and Indian Oceans. They live most of their adult lives in the shallow waters along coastlines.

serrated beak to cut through sea grasses and algae

dark on top to blend in with ocean floor

streamlined shell to move through water easily

paddles to propel through the water

quick exhalation and inhalation to replace air in lungs in one to three seconds

Rivers and Lakes

Freshwater rivers and lakes are found all over the world, in both warm and cold climates. Rivers usually contain moving water, while the water in most lakes is still.

River movement

The source of a river is usually a lake or underground spring in high ground. As a river gets further from its source, it widens, and its water becomes warmer and murkier. The movement of water along a river carves a channel through the land, with banks on either side.

source

mouth

Lake Superior in North America is the largest freshwater lake on Earth.

Lakes

Lakes are large bodies of freshwater that are surrounded by land. Some lakes are isolated, while others are connected by rivers. In cold areas, the top layer of a lake can freeze in winter.

Banks

River and lake banks are usually muddy, as water mixes with soil from the land. Animals such as water voles and catfish live in holes in the banks. Reeds and cattails grow in the muddy soil. Herons and storks wade in the shallow water, hunting fish and frogs.

River life

In both rivers and lakes, algae and insects live on the sunny surface of the water. Fish live in the warm water close to the surface, while crustaceans such as crayfish live on the muddy river bed. Some lakes are so deep that the water at the bottom is cold and pitch-black.

Lake Baikal in Russia is the world's deepest lake. Its deepest point is 5,387 feet (1,642 m), twice the height of the tallest building on Earth—the Burj Khalifa in Dubai.

Animal and plant adaptations

River animals need to be adapted for moving water. Some are streamlined so that the current washes over them smoothly, while others shelter on or cling to rocks. It can be hard for freshwater plants to photosynthesize underwater, which is why many plants grow out of the water.

Frogs have strong back legs to push them forward in the water, even against the current.

The river otter has sensitive whiskers that can feel the movements of prey, making it easier to hunt in **murky** water.

Water lilies have their roots in the river or lake bed, but grow long stems and large leaves that float on the surface of the water, where there is more light.

27

The Nile River

The Nile is the longest river in the world. It flows north through northeast Africa and passes through ten countries, including Uganda, Sudan, and Egypt.

FACT FILE

LENGTH
4,132 miles (6,650 km)

AVERAGE WIDTH
1,7 MILES (2.8 km)

AVERAGE DEPTH
26 to 36 feet (8 to 11 m)

Tributaries

The Nile has two **tributaries**–the Blue Nile, which starts in Lake Victoria, and the White Nile, which starts in Lake Tana in Ethiopia. The two rivers meet in Sudan, forming the main section of the Nile, which continues north to the Nile **Delta**.

Some sections of the Nile have fast-moving rapids and waterfalls, such as Murchison Falls, which is found on the White Nile in Uganda.

Delta

In the north of Egypt, the Nile River splits into several smaller rivers as it moves toward the Mediterranean Sea. The swampy area between the small rivers, known as the delta, attracts much wildlife, including hundreds of thousands of birds.

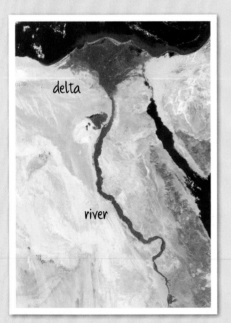

delta

river

The lush Nile delta and the green, fertile land on the river banks can be seen from space.

River banks

The Nile and its tributaries pass through areas of rain forest, savanna, and desert. In desert areas, the river **irrigates** the dry river banks, making them lush and fertile and attractive to plants and wildlife.

Flooding

In the past, the Nile would flood every year, leaving fertile mud on the river banks and making it suitable for farming. The construction of the Aswan Dam in the 1950s stopped the flooding of the Nile. Today, farmers use artificial fertilizers on their fields.

The Nile passes through Cairo, the capital city of Egypt.

People

The Nile was key to the development of the ancient Egyptian civilization. Farmers grew crops on the banks of the river and boats were used to transport goods between cities. Today, there are many settlements along the river, including large cities such as Khartoum and Juba.

Nile crocodile

The Nile crocodile lurks in shallow water. It has no known predators and finds plenty of prey in and around the water.

very powerful jaw and conical teeth so that prey can't escape from its strong grip

stomach can digest almost anything, including bones, hooves, and shells

protective membranes on eyes so that it can open its eyes underwater

nostrils on top of the head to breathe while hiding underwater

29

Glossary

adapted Changed over time to be well-suited to surroundings

antifreeze A liquid that stops other liquids from freezing

biodiverse Describes an area that has a high number of species of living things

biomes Natural areas on Earth that have the same climate, landscape, plants, and animals

camouflage The coloring of an animal that helps it to blend in with its surroundings

current A movement of water in one direction

deciduous Describes a tree that loses its leaves in autumn and regrows them in spring

delta An area at the mouth of a river where it splits into smaller streams

ecosystem The relationship between all living things in an area

endangered Describes a species that is seriously at risk of extinction

evaporated Turned from a liquid into a gas

evergreen Describes a tree that has green leaves all year round

fertile Describes land where plants can grow well

glacier A large mass of ice that moves slowly

habitat The area where a certain plant or animal lives

hibernate To go into a sleep-like state for the winter and wake up in spring

Indigenous Describes peoples that originally lived in a place

irrigate To bring water to an area of land

migration The movement of animals from one place to another at the same time every year

murky Dark and not clear

oasis A small, fertile area surrounded by desert

omnivore An animal that eats both animals and plants

photosynthesize To make energy from sunlight, carbon dioxide, and water

plateau A large, high, flat area of land

predator An animal that hunts a weaker or smaller animal

prey An animal that is hunted by a predator

settlement A place where humans have settled, such as a town

streamlined Describes something with a smooth shape that water or air can pass over easily

tributary A river or stream that flows into a larger river

Test yourself!

1. Which forest biome mainly has evergreen trees?
2. Name an animal that lives in the rainforest canopy.
3. On which continent is the Serengeti?
4. Name two ways in which camels are adapted to the desert.
5. Why do many tundra animals migrate?
6. Why do ocean mammals have large lungs?
7. Is coral a plant or an animal?
8. Where is the Nile Delta?

Check your answers on page 32.

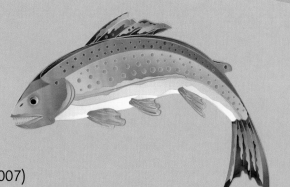

Further reading

Biomes and Ecosystems
Barbara J. Davis (Gareth Stevens, 2007)

***Earth's Natural Biomes* series**
(Crabtree Publishing, 2018)

***Ecosystems Inside Out* series**
(Crabtree Publishing, 2015)

Websites

Read more about biomes at the following websites:

www.ucmp.berkeley.edu/glossary/gloss5/biome/

www.cotf.edu/ete/modules/msese/earthsysflr/biomes.html

www.earthobservatory.nasa.gov/Experiments/Biome/

Index

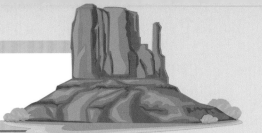

Answers

1 Taiga

2 Some animals include the toucan and the spider monkey.

3 Africa

4 Wide hooves to balance on sand, thick lips to eat thorny desert plants, thick eyelashes to stop sand entering the eye, hump that stores energy.

5 Because the winter there is too cold for them to survive.

6 So that they can spend more time underwater before coming to the surface to breathe.

7 An animal

8 On the Mediterranean Sea, on the north coast of Egypt.